Record-Breaking Bugs
AMAZING INSECTS

By Matt Turner

Illustrated by Santiago Calle

HUNGRY
TOMATO™

RECORD-BREAKING BUGS
AMAZING
INSECTS

Thanks to the creative team:
Senior Editor: Alice Peebles
Fact checking: Kate Mitchell
Designer: www.collaborate.agency

First published in Great Britain in 2016
by Hungry Tomato Ltd
PO Box 181
Edenbridge
Kent, TN8 9DP
Copyright © 2016 Hungry Tomato Ltd

A CIP catalogue record for this book is
available from the British Library.
ISBN 978-1-910684-68-9

Printed and bound in China

Discover more at
www.hungrytomato.com

CONTENTS

Extraordinary Insects

We humans may think we rule the planet, but actually the insects are in charge!

For a start, they outnumber us. At a rough guess there are ten quintillion (10,000,000,000,000,000,000) insects alive at any one time, made up of more than 900,000 species. And they're far older than us, going back nearly 400 million years, long before the dinosaur age. They're about 120 million years older than the flowering plants, too. In other words, flowering plants evolved to survive alongside existing insects, rather than the other way around.

Some insects live alone, but the more advanced – ants, bees, termites – form complex societies, working together to build megastructures, gather food, nurse their young, and defeat enemies.

This book looks at some of the most amazing adaptations of modern insects: their beauty, camouflage, engineering skills, senses, weapons, defences and sneaky survival tricks, plus some of the ways – both welcome and otherwise – they affect humanity. And the great thing about them is you have an insect zoo in your house and garden. Go take a look…

GREAT SURVIVORS

A cockroach can live for weeks without its head. And the severed head can keep on waving its antennae for hours!

Cockroaches first appeared about 320 million years ago. Modern-day roaches developed about 200 million years ago and walked with the dinosaurs.

Cockroaches are scavengers. In a pinch they will eat just about anything: glue, grease, soap, wallpaper paste, leather, bookbindings or even hair.

Some roaches are big. *Megaloblatta longipennis* boasts a 17.5-cm (7-in) wingspan; the Australian rhino cockroach can weigh 33.5 g (well over 1 oz).

Cockroaches are fast! Once all six legs are in motion, a roach can sprint at speeds of up to 1.5 m (59 in) per second. And they're elusive, too, with the ability to 'turn on a dime' while in full stride.

COCKROACHES

Flick on the kitchen light at night, and you may see a flat brown insect racing over the floor to a dark hiding-place. Few insects are so unloved as the cockroach – but, of about 4,600 known species, only 30 or so are pests. Some are specially adapted for cold or dry habitats, but most are generalized, eat-anything, go-anywhere critters… which helps explain how roaches are found in almost every corner of the planet.

MADAGASCAR HISSING COCKROACH
GROMPHADORHINA PORTENTOSA
Size: up to 76 mm (3 in)
Lifespan: 2–5 years

NUCLEAR PROOF
In a nuclear attack, among the survivors would be fruit flies and cockroaches. They can handle mega-doses of radiation that would kill humans.

SWEET TOOTH
If a cockroach is introduced to a sweet taste, such as vanilla or peppermint, it will drool in anticipation when it later detects the scent in the air.

WORKING TOGETHER

Worker ants of all sizes cooperate. Left: An *Atta* major carries a leaf fragment, giving minors a ride; in return, they guard her from parasitic flies. Centre: A *Pheidologeton* supermajor acts as a 'troop transport' for minors. Right: An army worker grooms a soldier's jaws.

A weaver ant gently holds a larva and taps it with its antennae to make it release silk. The ant uses the silk to stick leaves together and build a colony home.

A queen driver ant is so big – up to 5 cm (2 in) long – that her tiny workers, just one-tenth her size, have to push her around.

Some workers in carpenter ant colonies take defence to the limit. When attacked, they explode and die, blasting toxic gunk all over their enemies.

Honeypot ant workers, or repletes, hang from the ceiling of the nest and regurgitate liquid sugar and protein from their abdomen to feed the other ants.

ANTS

Ants are found worldwide, having evolved only about 130 million years ago from ancient wasps. They form colonies, sometimes millions strong, made up of several castes – queen, worker, soldier, and so on – all performing different roles. They work together to build the nest, raise the young and fend off enemies. Ants will fight to the death for the colony's survival.

AUSTRALIAN BULLDOG ANT
MYRMECIA BREVINODA
Size: worker 17–26 mm (0.6–1 in)
Lifespan: up to 2 years approx.

FIERCE
A bulldog ant is so fierce that, if it is cut in two, the head will still try to bite the abdomen, and the abdomen will sting the head.

HEAVY
If you took a giant set of scales to the Brazilian Amazon rainforest and put all the ants on one side, and all of the other land vertebrates (mammals, birds, reptiles and amphibians) on the other, the ants would be four times heavier.

Fearsome Larvae

Antlions are holometabolous: they go through a complete egg-larva-pupa-adult life cycle. First, a female lacewing deposits eggs in dirt or sand.

The hatched larva digs a cone-shaped pit, burying itself at the bottom, but leaving its long, toothed jaws free. Then it lies in wait.

If prey tumbles in, the antlion may flick sand up to cause a 'sandslide', knocking the victim off its feet. Bursting out from its hiding-place, the antlion uses the hollow teeth of its jaws first to inject its victim with digestive venom, then to suck out the resulting 'soup', leaving nothing but an empty husk.

The larva pupates inside a round cocoon about the size of a chickpea. It may remain here, buried in sand, for several years.

Finally, the long, slender, winged adult hatches from the pupa. It spends the next few weeks searching for a mate, and not feeding at all.

ANTLIONS

Antlions are not ants, but lacewings, with about 2,000 species found worldwide. While the adult is a winged insect that looks like a rather scrawny dragonfly, the larva is a more fearsome beast. And while sometimes it simply hides among leaves or in rock cracks, it is best known for its habit of digging a sandpit, where it lurks with jaws gaping wide, waiting to capture prey and suck it dry.

ANTLION
MYRMELEON SP.
Size: larva up to 15 mm (0.6 in),
adult up to 80 mm (3.1 in)
Lifespan: larva 3 years or more,
adult 25–45 days

SNEAKY
The name 'antlion' is centuries old. Maurus, a medieval scholar, said of the larva that 'it conceals itself in dust and kills ants that carry provisions'.

NICKNAME
Some Americans call antlions 'doodlebugs'. In *Tom Sawyer*, the classic tale by Mark Twain, Tom talks to a doodlebug to coax it out of its hole.

Borers and Battlers

These are male giraffe weevils (*Lasiorhynchus barbicornis*) from New Zealand. They look rather different from the Madagascar giraffe weevil opposite, but they probably fight the same 'snout battles' to decide who mates with females. Their huge snouts measure up to half the male's total length of 8 cm (3.25 in).

In the acorn weevil it's the female who has the longer snout. She uses it to bore a hole in an acorn, then turns around and lays an egg in it.

The larva develops inside the acorn, then drills its way out and drops into the soil, where it pupates for a year or two before becoming an adult.

The palm weevil lays up to 500 eggs at a time in coconut, date and oil palms. Its big larvae chew through the timber, ruining the crops.

Insects are rich in protein. In Malaysia, people cook weevils in a dish called 'Sago Delight'. In Vietnam, weevils dipped in fish sauce are eaten alive. Mmm!

WEEVILS

Weevils are smallish beetles, usually with a long snout, and their antennae have an 'elbow' joint. There are over 60,000 known species, and although farmers hate them because they burrow into plants and damage crops, weevils have some fascinating adaptations. In some species the snout – or rostrum – reaches extraordinary lengths, and males use theirs to battle each other over females.

MADAGASCAR GIRAFFE WEEVIL
TRACHELOPHORUS GIRAFFA
Size: up to 25 mm (1 in)
Lifespan: 1 year approx.

QUANTITY
Nearly one in four of all life forms is a beetle – and of these, around one in five is a weevil. Beetles are everywhere!

WELL-NAMED
The male Madagascar giraffe weevil is nearly all neck! After mating, the female (which has a much shorter neck) carefully lays her eggs in rolled-up leaves, one egg per leaf.

INCREDIBLE HULKS

Giant weta regularly weigh 35 g (1.25 oz), more than a mouse. The heaviest on record – a pregnant female – tipped the scales at 70 g (2.5 oz).

Like her cousins the crickets, the female weta has a spiked ovipositor, which she uses for laying eggs. She pushes the eggs into damp soil.

The mountain weta lives high above the snowline. It can survive being frozen stiff! It just thaws out in warmer weather... and carries on.

Tusked weta were discovered in 1970. Males use their tusks in jousting battles over females, and rub them together to make a rasping noise.

Cave weta aren't giants, but they do have long legs, which may span up to 21 cm (8.25 in) on a body just 3.5 cm (1.4 in) long. You can find lots of them clinging to the roofs of cool, damp caves in New Zealand, so if you go looking for them, remember to check your coat collar afterwards! They're good at jumping, too.

GIANT WETA

A flightless vegetarian with a face like a samurai warrior, armed with powerful jaws and spiky legs… and heavier than a sparrow? Meet the giant weta! All 11 species live in New Zealand, where rats, stoats and other introduced predators have wiped out their mainland populations, leaving the only survivors on islands or reserves. There are smaller weta species, too, living in caves, forests and even high mountains.

GIANT WETA
GENUS: *DEINACRIDA*
Size: up to 10 cm (4 in)
Weight: up to 70 g (2.5 oz)
Lifespan: 2 years

ISLAND GIANTS
Giant weta are examples of island gigantism: animals or plants that evolve in isolation on islands can, over time, become enormous.

UGLY
The Maori people of New Zealand named this insect *wetapunga*, after the god of ugly things, or *taipo*, meaning 'ghost' or 'spook'.

LEAF LOOKALIKES

Antonio Pigafetta found leaf insects when he explored the Philippines in 1519–22. He thought they were 'walking leaves' that fed on air.

Nymphs (young) shed their skin several times as they grow. If they lose a leg or antenna, they can regrow it – the limb gets bigger with each moult.

Phasmids have amazing night vision. With each moult, the eyes grow bigger, but more sensitive. So while nymphs come out by day, adults are mostly nocturnal.

Some leaf insects spray a defensive fluid from glands in their neck, to stop predators bothering them. If it gets in your eyes, it's very painful.

Relatives of the leaf insects include the two-striped walkingstick or 'devil rider', an American species. The male and female are usually found attached together in summer and autumn when mating. They go everywhere together and they don't separate until one of the pair dies and drops off!

LEAF INSECTS

The leaf insects or 'walking leaves' have taken camouflage to the absolute limit, with bodies that have evolved to look exactly like real leaves. They have veins and ribs, and even crinkly brown edges. Related to stick insects, they are known as phasmids. Like some wasp species, leaf insect females can produce eggs without the help of a male, and the eggs hatch… into more females!

GIANT LEAF INSECT
PHYLLIUM GIGANTEUM
Size: up to 11 cm (4.3 in)
Lifespan: 5–7 months

RARE MALE
There are male leaf insects, but they're incredibly rare. The first male giant leaf insect was only discovered as late as 1994.

CANNIBAL
Stick insects make great pets. But if they run out of leaves to eat, they'll eat leaf insects instead… so you can't keep two together in one cage!

Cool Camouflage

The mantis is the only insect able to move its head through 180° each way. So it can perch stock-still and keep watching prey carefully.

The two dots that 'float' around the eyes are false pupils: the part of each eye that absorbs light while the rest of the eye is reflecting it.

Like the leaf insects, mantises walk in a wobbly way. They do this for an extra camouflage effect, swaying like a twig in a breeze. The flower mantis on the left, however, is putting on a deimatic display – a startling move that shows off its bright colours. It sometimes does this to scare off predators.

Insect camouflage reaches beautiful extremes in species like the orchid mantises. They're hard to pick out from the flowers on which they lurk!

The mantis egg sac, or ootheca, looks like a squeeze of toothpaste, often fastened to a garden fence. Newly hatched nymphs look just like mini mantises.

MANTISES

The mantis is an ambush expert, a predator so well-camouflaged it melts into the scenery when perched on a plant. The big compound eyes watch for movement, and if another insect settles near, the mantis flicks out its long, spiked forelegs to snatch it. The many different species show wonderful variations of camouflage – some look like colourful flowers, others like rotten leaves or dry twigs.

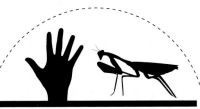

VIOLIN MANTIS
GONGYLUS GONGYLODES
Size: female 10 cm (4 in),
male 8–9 cm (3.1–3.5 in)
Lifespan: 1 year,
sometimes 2

THORNY
The violin mantis has an extra-long thorax, which resembles the slender neck of a fiddle. It also looks just like the dry twigs of rose bushes, where it likes to hide.

VANISHING ACT
A young mantis may change colour – from brown to green, say – when moulting, in order to blend more closely with its environment.

GLOWING IN THE DARK

A male *Photinus* firefly flashes a special pattern to attract a female of the same species, who then flashes a 'Come here!' answer that leads him to her.

Sometimes, a sneaky female from the genus *Photuris* tricks a *Photinus* male by flashing the correct answer... and then eats him when he finds her!

The New Zealand glow-worm is the cave-dwelling larva of a fly. It lives in a 'sleeping bag' of mucus, slung from the roof on lines of silk. The larva spins silken threads up to 50 cm (20 in) long, covered with beads of sticky mucus. Then it 'switches on' the bioluminescent light at its back end...

Any flying insect that bumps into a dangling thread is instantly trapped by the mucus; now the glow-worm larva reels it up and eats it.

In America, some beetle larvae glow to lure prey, such as millipedes. They are known as 'railroad worms' because they look like a train lit up at night.

GLOW-WORMS and FIREFLIES

Glow-worms and fireflies can give out light, like a living torch. There are over 2,000 species: some shine to warn predators they taste bad, while others do it to attract a mate, or to lure prey. The natural light, or bioluminescence, comes from a chemical reaction in the abdomen. It's similar to what happens when you crack a glow-stick – except that the glow-worm can keep doing it.

COMMON GLOW-WORM
LAMPYRIS NOCTILUCA
Size: larva 3–25 mm (0.1 in–1 in),
adult 15–30 mm (0.6 in–1.2 in)
Lifespan: larva 2–2 ½ years,
adult 10–16 days

EFFICIENT
Glow-worm bioluminescence is a 'cold' light. Almost 100 per cent of the energy used is converted to light, with none wasted as heat.

LIGHT DISPLAY
Sometimes all the fireflies in one area will flash on and off at the same time, in a huge synchronized display. No one (except the fireflies) is quite sure why.

Beetle Defences

The bombardier beetle mixes chemicals in its abdomen to blast out a shot of scalding-hot poison, harming or even killing would-be predators.

Ladybirds ooze haemolymph from their limb joints, which not only tastes bad but also hardens on air contact, gluing up the jaws of attackers.

The palmetto tortoise beetle larva (left) hides in a 'tent' made from strings of its own poos. The adult beetle (centre) has big feet, each with 10,000 bristles and glands that can ooze a gluey oil. When threatened, it glues its feet to the floor (such as a leaf) and becomes impossible to dislodge (right).

If it crash-lands on water, the rove beetle *Stenus comma* skates away using 'fart power'. Gases released from special glands jet-propel it to a safe place.

Carrion beetles (and their larvae) feed on decaying animal carcasses – really dirty places! They give off ammonia to keep free of harmful bacteria.

BEETLES

There are more species of beetle than of any other animal group on Earth. Many are eaten as prey, turning up on the menu of birds, lizards, mammals, insects and spiders, so they've evolved an arsenal of spectacular defences, including deadly poisons, explosions, cleaning fluids and jet propulsion. Even the humble garden ladybird can squeeze out something nasty to defend itself!

ROVE BEETLE
FAMILY: STAPHYLINIDAE
Size: <1–40 mm
(<0.03 in–1.6 in)
Lifespan: adult 20–60 days

EVOLUTION
Chemical defences of one kind or another have evolved more than 30 times during the 270-million-year history of beetles.

TOXIC
The haemolymph (blood) of some rove beetles contains pederin, a super-deadly toxin that is thought to deter predatory spiders.

BIG BUILDERS

Welcome to termite society! The queen, tended by a king, spends her long life laying eggs. Workers and soldiers are blind and cannot reproduce. Every so often, the queen produces some alates: these are winged termites that breed to start new colonies. In the picture above, can you work out who's who?

Termites are architects and farmers! Some termites build huge mud towers, complete with basements, air-conditioning ducts and fungus farms.

Soldiers defend the colony. Some have jaws, but this is a nasute: a soldier with a nozzle-like head for squirting toxic goo at ants and other enemies.

Drywood termites are a pest, living in our walls, chewing the timbers and causing billions of dollars' worth of damage worldwide each year.

TERMITES

Termites are tiny social insects with a huge impact. Some species ruin houses and crops, but many others are the farmer's friend, improving the soil surrounding their massive colonies, which contain thousands, even millions of workers and soldiers, all slaving together in blind obedience to the queen (pictured below). And what a queen! Measuring up to 10 cm (4 in) long, she may live to be 50 years old – an insect record.

TERMITES
ORDER: ISOPTERA
Size: workers 4–15 mm (0.15–0.6 in), queen up to 100 mm (4 in) or more
Lifespan: workers and soldiers 1–2 years, queen up to 50 years

MINI-COWS
Termites have been referred to as 'mini-cows' because their multi-chambered gut can break down cellulose, the tough stuff in plants.

FOOD CHAIN
Winged termites provide more food for the mammals, birds and amphibians of tropical forests than any other insect group.

RECORD-BREAKING INSECTS

Insects may be small, but they notch up some fascinating records. You won't find the biggest, deadliest, fastest insects on these two pages: instead, here are some feats that relate to the book. Also, you can study some of these insects in the house and garden – although hopefully there are no termites hiding in your walls!

Night light: The brightest bioluminescent insect is the Jamaican click beetle. The light comes from two 'headlights' on the top of its thorax, as well as a glowing patch on the underside of the abdomen. The light is so bright that local people used to collect the beetles in gourds and hang them from the ceiling to illuminate their huts.

Hello there!

Changeling: The insect that undergoes the greatest number of moults is the silverfish. This ancient creature, little changed since the dinosaur era, gets into our homes and nibbles our books and clothes. It may shed its exoskeleton 60 times or more.

Supercolony: The largest ant colony found to date was in southern Europe, made up of 30 linked colonies across an area 6,000 km (3,700 miles) wide. It contained untold billions of workers. Incredibly, there is also a 'megacolony' of Argentine ants living in far-flung lands, from California to Europe and Japan. Unrelated ants will usually fight, but ants from these different groups act friendly when brought together, proving their kinship.

A rovin': Talking of big families… the largest of all animal families is the Staphylinidae or rove beetle family. It contains more than 62,000 named species, and there are plenty more to discover. In fact, there are more species of rove beetle than of all the vertebrates (animals with backbones) put together.

High-rise: The tallest insect-built structures, relative to insect body length, are the termite mounds in Africa, some measuring up to 9 m (29 ft) tall. In human terms, that's like a mile-high skyscraper. What's more, termite nests can extend deep below ground… to more than 60 m (200 ft) in some cases!

AMAZING INSECT FEATS

What do you call a fly with no wings?

A walk! Actually, there are lots of wingless flies. They include the snow flies in the genus *Chionea*, which – as their name suggests – can be found in winter, walking on snow. Their haemolymph (blood) contains a natural antifreeze. Other wingless examples include bat flies – true flies that live as parasites on the fur of bats, and can only take flight by hitching a ride.

Can insect poisons save human lives?

Scientists are studying several insect poisons for use in anti-cancer drugs. These poisons include pederin (see page 25), as well as DHMA, a rare fatty acid found in soldier beetles. Another is MP1, a toxin from the venom of a Brazilian wasp, which seems to kill cancer cells while leaving normal cells unharmed.

How many ants are there?

At any one time, there are about a quadrillion of them – 1,000,000,000,000,000 – on Earth.

Can goats rescue insects?

Introduced rats, stoats and other predators killed so many giant weta in New Zealand that the insects were believed extinct on the mainland. Then in 1962, giant weta were discovered in a clump of spiky gorse bushes near Mahoenui in the North Island. They had survived because the grazing of goats had kept the gorse growth so dense that rats couldn't penetrate it. More than 50 years on, the weta are still there.

GLOSSARY

abdomen — the hind part of an insect's three-part body (along with the head and thorax).

antennae — the two 'feelers' on an insect's head, providing touch, taste and smell.

caste — in insects that form societies, such as ants, bees, wasps and termites, a caste is a social group, such as a worker or soldier.

cocoon — in insects that undergo complete metamorphosis, the cocoon is the casing around a pupa, inside which an insect larva gradually transforms into an adult.

gland — an organ that can produce a chemical and release it, either into the body or outside it.

introduced predators — predatory animals brought (intentionally or otherwise) by humans from their native range into a foreign range. They often upset the local ecosystem.

invertebrate — an animal without a backbone, such as spiders, insects, crustaceans and myriapods.

mandibles — jaws.

metamorphosis — the process in which an animal, such as a butterfly, goes through a number of life stages, including egg, larva/nymph, pupa, adult. Some insects skip the pupal stage.

millisecond — one-thousandth of a second.

moult — in insects, to shed the hard exoskeleton (outer part) in order to grow. The new exoskeleton is soft but hardens after moulting.

ovipositor — a hollow, often spike-like organ on a female's abdomen, which she uses to lay eggs.

predator — an animal that kills and eats other animals. Roughly one-third of all insect species are predatory.

pupa — a stage of metamorphosis in which the insect larva rests inside a case and gradually transforms into an adult.

regurgitate — to 'sick up' digested food from the stomach. Ants, for instance, often feed one another on regurgitated food.

rostrum — the snout or beak of an insect, such as a beetle.

scavenger — an animal that feeds on whatever it can find, such as fallen fruit, carrion (dead animal remains) or garbage.

thorax — the middle part of an insect's three-part body (between the head and abdomen).

venom — poison that is injected (from an ant's stinger, for example) into prey or an enemy.

Hello, little dude!

INDEX

The Author

British-born Matt Turner graduated from Loughborough College of Art in the 1980s, since which he has worked as a picture researcher, editor and writer. He has authored books on diverse topics including natural history, earth sciences and railways, as well as hundreds of articles for encyclopedias and partworks, covering everything from elephants to abstract art. He and his family currently live in Auckland, Aotearoa/New Zealand, where he volunteers for the local Coastguard unit and dabbles in painting.

The Artist

Born in Medellin, Colombia, Santiago Calle is an illustrator and animator trained at Edinburgh College of Art in the UK. He began his career as a teacher, which led him to deepen his studies in sequential art. Santiago founded his art studio Liberum Donum in Bogotá in 2006, partnering with his brother Juan. Since then, they have dedicated themselves to producing concept art, illustration, comic strip art and animation.